Giraffe in the bath

Russell Punter

Illustrated by David Semple

Giraffe's in her garden.

She tugs up thick weeds...

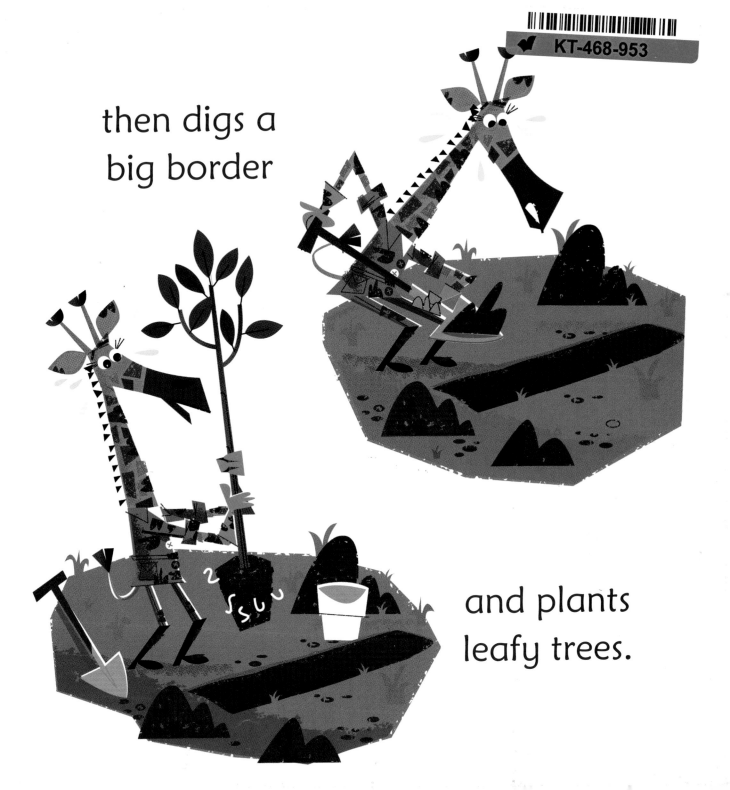

then digs a
big border

and plants
leafy trees.

Giraffe is tired out.

She trots up the path.

"Now I'm grubby and muddy.
I need a hot bath."

She jumps in the tub,
with a splish and a splosh.

The bubbles float upwards.
She gets set to wash...

The phone goes...

RING RING!

She runs to reply.

Then three minutes later...
'Knock, knock!'
at the door.

Giraffe tries to relax,
with her eyes tightly shut.

But Baboon backs his truck...

...through the side of her hut!

The bathtub goes sliding,
through slippery soap.

It glides out of the door,
down a really steep slope.

"Look out!" shouts Giraffe,
her voice all a-quiver.

Ten zebras take cover,
as she heads to the river.

With a crash and a splash,
Giraffe lands by a raft.

Soon her bathtub is bobbing
past lots of odd craft.

She floats over the line
in the Big Bathtub Race.

FINISH LINE

"What a win!" cries the judge.
"Here's your prize for first place!"

About phonics

Phonics is a method of teaching reading used extensively in today's schools. At its heart is an emphasis on identifying the *sounds* of letters, or combinations of letters, that are then put together to make words. These sounds are known as phonemes.

Starting to read
Learning to read is an important milestone for any child. The process can begin well before children start to learn letters and put them together to read words. The sooner children can discover books and enjoy stories and language, the better they will be prepared for reading themselves, first with the help of an adult and then independently.

You can find out more about phonics on the Usborne Very First Reading website, **www.usborne.com/veryfirstreading** (US readers go to **www.veryfirstreading.com**). Click on the **Parents** tab at the top of the page, then scroll down and click on **About synthetic phonics**.

Phonemic awareness

An important early stage in pre-reading and early reading is developing phonemic awareness: that is, listening out for the sounds within words. Rhymes, rhyming stories and alliteration are excellent ways of encouraging phonemic awareness.

In this story, your child will soon identify the *a* sound, as in **giraffe** and **bath**. Look out, too, for rhymes such as **crash** – **splash** and **race** – **place**.

Hearing your child read

If your child is reading a story to you, don't rush to correct mistakes, but be ready to prompt or guide if he or she is struggling. Above all, do give plenty of praise and encouragement.

Edited by Jenny Tyler
Designed by Hope Reynolds

Reading consultants: Alison Kelly and Anne Washtell

First published in 2017 by Usborne Publishing Ltd., Usborne House, 83-85 Saffron Hill, London EC1N 8RT, England.
www.usborne.com Copyright © 2017 Usborne Publishing Ltd.